Eugene MAGALIF

Revelation
for Flute and Piano

For Sir James Galway

Southern®
MUSIC

For Sir James Galway

REVELATION

Eugene Magalif, ASCAP

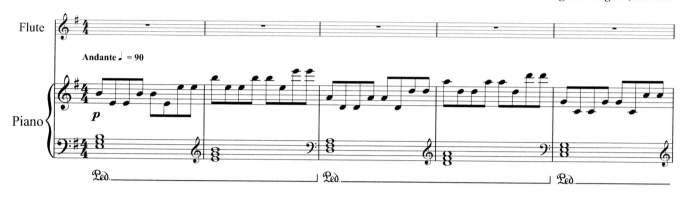

4

Eugene MAGALIF

Revelation
for Flute and Piano

For Sir James Galway

Flute

For Sir James Galway

REVELATION

Andante ♩ = 90

Eugene Magalif, ASCAP

Copyright © 2017 Southern Music Company (ASCAP)

3

Flute

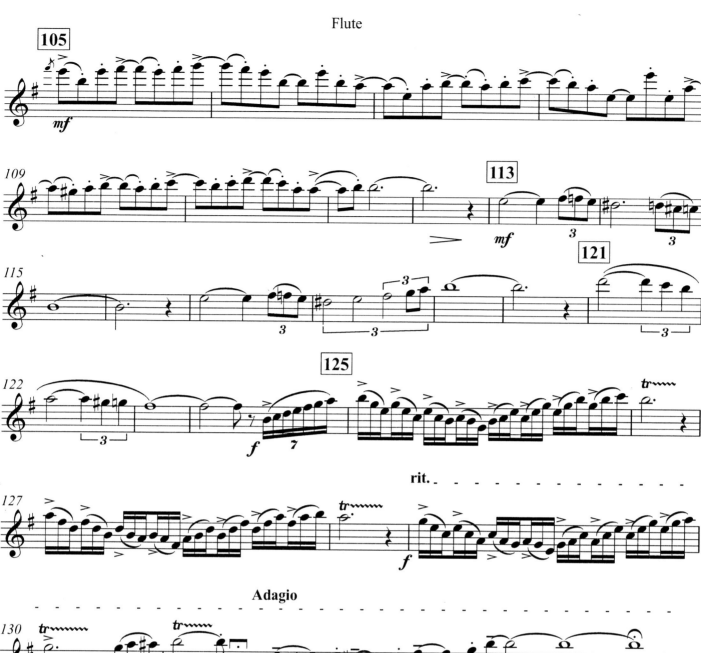